Secrets To Landing

Corporate Sponsorships

The Insider's Playbook to Landing Large Checks from Big Companies

Shayna Rattler

www.becomeasponsorshipmagnet.com

Self Published 2018 | Texas, United States
Copyright 2018 Shayna Rattler

All rights reserved. No part of this book may be reproduced in any form or by any electronic or mechanical means - except in the case of brief quotations embodied in articles or reviews - without written permission from its author.

ISBN 978-1985627130
DALLAS, TX

The information presented herein represents the view of the author as of the date of publication. Because of the rate with which conditions change, the author reserves the right to alter and update her opinion based on the new conditions. This book is for informational purposes only. While every attempt has been made to verify the information provided in this book, neither the author nor her affiliates/partners assume any responsibility for errors, inaccuracies or omissions. Any slights of people or organizations are unintentional. You should be aware of any laws, which govern business transactions or other business practices in your country and state. Any reference to any person or business whether living or dead is purely coincidental.

Every effort has been made to accurately represent this idea and its potential. Examples in these materials are not to be interpreted as a promise or guarantee of earnings. Earning potential is entirely dependent on the person using our programs, ideas and techniques. We do not purport this as a "get rich scheme."

Your level of success in attaining the results claimed in my materials depends on the time you devote to the programs, ideas and techniques mentioned, your finances, knowledge and various skills. Since these factors differ according to individuals, I cannot guarantee your success or income level. Nor am I responsible for any of your actions.

Any and all forward looking statements here or on any of my sales material are intended to express my opinion of earnings potential. Many factors will be important in determining your actual results and no guarantees are made that you will achieve results similar to ours or anybody else's, in fact no guarantees are made that you will achieve any results from my ideas and techniques in my material.

ALL RIGHTS RESERVED. No part of this book may be reproduced or transmitted in any form whatsoever, electronic, or mechanical, including photocopying, recording, or by any informational storage or retrieval without the expressed written consent of the author.

To Every Entrepreneur and Influencer out there crushing it and making your dreams a reality. I celebrate you and what you're creating in the world…

What Shayna's Clients *(And Biggest Fans)* **Say...**

Shayna Rattler is who I turn to for corporate sponsorship advice. She knows exactly what big companies are looking for and provides great guidance for getting their attention on your brand. When you build a six and seven figure brand and are ready for bigger partnership opportunities, getting Shayna in your corner will be one of the best business decisions you make.
    ~ **Jennifer Kem** | www.jenniferkem.com

Shayna Rattler's corporate sponsorship strategies have taught me the effective ways to create a partnership opportunity. I've even gained the confidence to speak openly about partnering with other women's organizations. Before working with Shayna I did not know where to start. Now, I have 5 meetings on my calendar and already landed one partner to launch an upcoming event.
    ~ **Kimberly Thomas** | www.coachkimburke.com

Shayna has given me insight plus useful tools and strategies to pitch to sponsors with confidence. Her messages are always clear and to the point. No FLUFF, just real FACTS that bring real results. I have restructured my proposal packages in order to include my newfound information.
    ~ **Sierra Rainge** | www.sierrarainge.com

I could not believe the quality of the information I received just from tuning in to Shayna's periscope sessions. I recently hired a PR firm to assist me with securing sponsorships for my non-profit, and after listening to Shayna I immediately wanted to fire the firm. She gives away some very good tips that gave me some

really quick fixes that have had immediate impact on my presentations. I can only imagine what I would gain if I actually hired her. I hope to work with her soon!
    ~ **Pamela Ellis** | www.smahrtgirl.org

Shayna helped me see how I could translate my unique gifts, talents and intellectual property as a creative marketing professional into packages that companies would really benefit from, and pay handsomely for. She knows how to make you show up like someone to be taken seriously, even if you're a corporation of one.
    ~ **Lisa Rothstein** | www.lisarothstein.com

Shayna has successfully landed in kind and monetary corporate sponsorships for both my conference and charity ball. She has a knack for building relationships and is extremely detail oriented and efficient.
    ~ **Phillip Ashley Rix** | Phillip Ashley Chocolates

I hosted my first conference this year and Shayna secured 2 corporate sponsors for the event. While working with her she worked with me to create a strategy, communicated with me frequently and managed the entire process in a way that gave me extreme confidence in her abilities. She really knows her stuff. We have already begun to work on securing sponsorships for next year.
    ~ **Nicole Roberts Jones** | www.nicolerobertsjones.com

SPONSORSHIP MAGNET

In addition to this book, I have made available an extensive collection of advanced training videos, guides, tutorials, actionable tips, templates, scripts, checklists and community support at www.becomeasponsorshipmagnet.com

Sponsorship Magnet is the only program that provides the roadmap to becoming corporate sponsor ready so you can stop self-funding your business.

No more searching. No more wasting time. No more mindless stares at a blank screen hoping someone reads your proposal. No more trying to figure it out on your own, only to get told NO!

What's included in Sponsorship Magnet:

- ★ **4 Training Videos** with Shayna to help you master what to do before, during and after the sponsor pitch.

- ★ **Unlimited Support & Guidance** in a private Facebook group where Shayna answers all of your questions and you have access to group feedback and critique of your proposals.

- ★ **Templates & Word-for-Word Scripts:** Fast track your success with these fill-in templates and scripts…

Claim your spot in Sponsorship Magnet at
www.BecomeASponsorshipMagnet.com

#SponsorMe

Take a photo of yourself holding this book and post it on Instagram using the hashtag above!

Table of Contents

Foreword by Jennifer Kem — 11

How To Read "Secrets To Landing Corporate Sponsorships" — 13

My Promise To You: RESULTS... — 14

Welcome To Corporate Sponsorships... — 15

The Corporate Sponsor Manifesto... — 19

Chapter 1: From Riches to Rags...to Riches Again — 21

Chapter 2: It's Time To LEVERAGE! — 29

Chapter 3: How Sponsorable Are You? (Take The Test) — 37

Chapter 4: POSITION - Showcase Your Assets — 43

Chapter 5: PACKAGE - Exposure Beyond An Event — 49

Chapter 6: PITCH - Get Past The Gatekeeper And Get In The Door — 61

Chapter 7: Get Your "HECK YES!" Check — 71

Chapter 8: Case Study - Steve Harvey — 77

Chapter 9: Case Study – Nicole Roberts Jones — 79

Chapter 10: Case Study – Jerylen Daniels — 81

BONUS RESOURCE: 60 Day Checklist — 83

Foreword
By Jennifer Kem

As the creator of Master Brand and a business coach to women who are building six and seven figure empires, I can quickly recognize when someone is truly an expert and Shayna Rattler definitely fits that mold.

I have had the pleasure of knowing Shayna when we were on the support team of a major influencer, and now as her coach and consultant.

In my eighteen plus years helping to build successful brands, I see countless business owners attempt to do more and more each year just to "stay on top." They're always seeking new ways to bring people into their tribes, creating new ways to serve them, and make more money doing it.

Corporate sponsorship can put an end to this rat race and there is no better person to teach you the right way to land those checks than Shayna Rattler!

With more and more business owners and solutions coming on the scene every year, the noise in the marketplace is deafening. It is also getting harder and harder to compete for consumer dollars. Now is the time to create ultimate sustainability in your business by bringing in corporate dollars.

Shayna Rattler is the secret weapon for learning how to become attractive to corporate sponsors and the framework she teaches is easy to implement alongside the other strategies in your business.

In *Secrets to Landing Corporate Sponsorships*, Shayna has laid out the roadmap to becoming sponsor ready in a very easy to read and digestible way. If you do what she suggests you will definitely be on your way to tapping into the power of this new revenue model. I am personally at the point in my brand where I'm ready to leverage what I've created to bring in corporate sponsors and I wouldn't consider working with anyone other than Shayna to advise me along the way.

Jennifer Kem
Creator of Master Brand
CEO of KemmComm Media Group

How To Read: Secrets To Landing Corporate Sponsorships

To make sure you get the absolute best results from your copy of <u>Secrets to Landing Corporate Sponsorships</u>, I've set up some easy guidelines for you to follow.

Write in the margins
- Take notes. Write questions and insights you have as you're reading. Make this book work for you. If you have a digital version of this book, I'd suggest printing it out.

Turn off distractions
- Turn off your phone, put the kids to bed, play soft music, log out of Facebook, and give yourself a break from all the noise so you can focus on you and your business. **You deserve it.**

Read this book as if it were a devotional
- Read one chapter then read it again.
- Take notes and follow the instructions in each section.
- Share your notes and insights with your spouse, business partners, friends, or accountability partners.

Commit To Your Reading
- Don't be interested in success; be committed. Set time aside to read a chapter a day.

My Promise To You: RESULTS

Too many books try to motivate you with pages and pages of fluff. As a result, a lot of people are motivated but not enough are empowered to take the right course of action that will yield a measurable result.

You're reading this book so I'm going to assume you're already motivated. I'm going to focus on telling you exactly what to do, when to do it, and how to do it successfully.

You'll notice a blank box and instructions at the end of each section called "Brain Stops" designed to help you immediately apply what you're reading. Don't just read this book - make this book work for you.

I can't **guarantee** you results. That's up to you. But I can promise to do everything I can to help you get those results.

Welcome to Corporate Sponsorships

Welcome to the First Edition of **Secrets to Landing Corporate Sponsorships!**

You may be reading this book because you've built a successful business but you're tired of the constant "launch cycle" you go through every year.

Or maybe you want to stop funding your own business, allowing you to keep more of your bottom line.

Or maybe you're a non-profit and you have work to do and no resources to support your vision.

Whatever your reason, I'm glad you're here.

After spending years working with personal brands, corporate Fortune 500 companies, and nonprofits, I'm excited to release this in-depth step-by-step strategy guide designed to help you **"become sponsorable."**

Whether you're an…

- Author
- CEO
- Non-Profit Director
- Social Media Influencer
- Event Planner

- Coach
- Consultant
- Expert
- Church Leader
- Service Provider
- Brick and Mortar Business Owner
- Musical Artist
- Podcast Host
- Blogger
- Speaker

… you're in the right place.

There are a TON of resources online when it comes to landing a corporate sponsor. Most of it is wrong.

I know this because I've spent years working with companies and major influencers like Steve Harvey, Lisa Nichols, the Susan G Komen Foundation, UPS, Delta Airlines, State Farm and Mary Kay.

I've also worked with small to medium sized businesses and influencers only known in their niche who've applied the same framework and reached massive goals.

I've become the go-to matchmaker for top brands and influencers and I know what works and what doesn't.

Secrets to Landing Corporate Sponsors is all about teaching you how to…

1. **POSITION** your business and showcase your brand assets in a powerful and attractive way to corporations ready to sign large checks.

2. **PACKAGE** your business assets in a way that sponsors can't help but want part of the action.

3. **PITCH** your opportunity in a way that builds the right relationships and gets past the gatekeeper.

Let me be clear: this is the exact framework that works with large enterprises and small businesses.

Corporations set aside money *(to the tune of $22 Billion Dollars a year)* to give to other businesses so they can get exposure for their brand in a way they can't without YOU.

That's what this book is all about…

- Getting you a piece of this $22 billion dollar pie…
- Destroying the launch cycle you're caught up in…
- Freeing you up to do the things you love to do without having to worry about funding every venture you take…

On the next page, you'll find <u>The Corporate Sponsor Manifesto</u>. I created this manifesto to help you recognize the role, purpose and responsibilities of what it means to partner with large companies.

Let's get started.

Shayna

The Corporate Sponsor Manifesto

~

I am Sponsorable.

I've built a powerful brand.
I'm ready to level up.

Show me the money.
Because I have important work to do.

Created by Shayna Rattler

"If it's legal, it's sponsorable"

~Shayna Rattler

Chapter 1
From Riches To Rags...
to Riches Again

I'm accustomed to making great money!

I immediately began to earn $100,000 a year in 2004 when I graduated from therapy school.

Being the overachiever I am, I started a therapy staffing agency a year later in 2005 and shortly after opening our doors we were generating $30,000 per month, with very little overhead.

I guess you can say I was set up to think the business world would always be a cakewalk.

I was in my late 20's and seemed to have it all– the big fancy house, $65,000 Benz, and designer bags galore. It's no wonder that people were coming to me for advice on how to start and grow a business and my pastor was asking me to teach classes on the topic at church.

It was at this time in 2007 that I realized not only did I have a knack for teaching others what I had accomplished, I truly felt like it was God's calling on my life to do so. As a result, I closed my staffing agency and began to coach full time.

That's when it happened!

My income plummeted to almost nothing. I had very few clients, no real plan in place for getting any, and bills were piling up. It was then I realized I had a lot to learn about this coaching business.

Why weren't deals just falling in my lap like they did in healthcare?

Back then I was only selling to consumers and I quickly learned the average consumer does not value investing in themselves and of those that do, many do not have the funds to do so.

I had to figure something out. My savings was only going to last so long. In fact, it was almost depleted.

I was struggling to generate the revenues to have a thriving business to take care of my teenage son and me. We often found ourselves in situations where we had to choose between this OR that, where in the past we could have this AND that.

By 2013 I wouldn't answer my phone. I felt the pain in my stomach as I realized I was going to lose my house in a few short months. Reluctantly, I sat in my lawyer's office signing the papers filing for bankruptcy as an attempt to save our home; all while pretending to friends and family everything was fine and dandy.

Needless to say, I was at the end of my rope!

I asked myself questions like:
- What am I missing?
- What experience do I have that I'm overlooking?
- Should it really be this hard?
- Why does success seem to be coming so effortlessly to others?

It was while holding on to that rope that I was hit with an epiphany. But before I tell you what that epiphany was, lets fast forward to today.

Today I have a thriving business where I have successful programs for influencers and small business owners to help them attract corporate sponsors and training and consulting for corporations. I am also a sought after speaker and have been featured in major publications like the Wall Street Journal and Black Enterprise.

Today I can answer my phone without first checking the caller ID. Although I still do check it first because we all have that cousin that calls to borrow money (smile). I no longer have to live an "OR" lifestyle but am back to giving my son the "AND" lifestyle he had grown accustomed to.

So what was that epiphany I mentioned?

While I was learning major lessons about entrepreneurship, I discovered if you're going to have a successful business for the long haul…

…it is critical that you pick an audience who can afford your services and offer a solution to a problem THEY recognize they have and that they are willing to fix.

One day it dawned on me. Corporations value investing in their brand AND they have the money to do so. I just had to figure out how the heck did I get them to talk to me AND choose me?

After scouring the Internet just to come up with no substantial answers, enrolling in NUMEROUS programs and hiring coach after coach who had no clue how to access corporate clients, I realized at that time there was absolutely NO support for a business owner trying to sell to corporations.

I began to panic.

I had spent all of my savings and knew if I didn't figure out something fast I was going to be forced to go back to what I was doing before, which would kill me slowly every day…

After about 18-24 months of hearing "No!" I finally discovered what corporations are looking for in a small business (and what will drive them away).

That's what you're going to learn in this book.

Have I made it? Absolutely not. Do we ever?

But in the process of figuring this out I have made a ton of money for myself and have helped my clients do so as well.

I'm committed to showing you how you too can change your family tree forever by landing large checks from big companies.

Hence the very book you're holding in your hands.

Don't take 18-24 months to figure it out on your own. Learn from my mistakes and victories and shortcut your path to this AMAZING corporate cash!

BRAIN STOP: Take a moment of silence and consider...

Is this possible for me?

Do I really want to continue to operate my business as I have in the past, paying for it all myself? Or am I willing to do whatever is necessary to have something different?

You're getting started on a journey that has the potential to change your life and business forever!!

Get feedback and advanced strategies by joining Sponsorship Magnet at www.becomeasponsorshipmagnet.com

"Stop wondering. Start doing."

~Jennifer Kem

Chapter 2
It's Time To LEVERAGE!

Did you know the average millionaire has 3 - 7 different streams of income? Of course you do.

We're constantly being advised to create multiple revenue streams for maximum profits and sustainability.

Although that is excellent advice, the problem with most revenue streams is that it requires you to create something new, often from scratch.

The other issue that most influencers and business owners face is that we're self-funding everything in our business, or worse, we're not able to offer all of the products and services we desire because we lack the cash flow to do so.

As you're looking to grow your business and revenues there is a belief that it is necessary to do MORE year after year.

That actually could not be further from the truth!

Growth is not in doing more, it's in LEVERAGING your efforts. The best form of leverage available to influencers today is hands down corporate sponsorship because it's a $22 Billion per year and growing industry.

The statistics show that only 2% of small business owners break the million-dollar mark and of those who do, 56% of their revenue comes from corporate clients and corporate sponsors.

Need I say more? In addition to the extra income it provides, corporate sponsorship also gives you more overall impact and influence, which is equally important to most folks these days.

I'd like for you to stop for a moment and create a vision in your mind.

- What would bringing in JUST A FRACTION of $22 BILLION dollars do for your business and life?
- What could you begin to say YES to?
- What could you begin to say NO to, if you increased your revenue by $25,000-$250,000 using this strategy?

After a certain point in your business journey, the last thing you really want to do is create another program, launch, or product, but you know you need new revenue streams to keep moving forward.

That's what makes the strategy of landing corporate sponsors so darn sexy. You can increase your revenues for what you've ALREADY created!

And contrary to what most experts teach, you don't even have to have a live event to get a big check! In fact, in my experience and that of my clients, it's easier to get a corporation to cut you a $25,000 check than it is to get an entrepreneur to pay $49 for an e-course…

The sad news is that 95% of influencers who are attempting to land corporate sponsors are being told NO, because they're focusing on all of the wrong things. This is mainly because there is outdated and even inaccurate information out there on how to do this right.

It's my mission to change the game on this so more influencers can tap into this misunderstood, yet lucrative revenue stream and create thriving businesses that positively impact the world.

If you've been concerned in the past with wanting to land corporate sponsors but don't know where to start or you have attempted and failed, if you don't know what to offer a potential sponsor, or don't know what to say when you do get in the door…

I HAVE YOU COVERED.

My goal in this book is to help you:

1. Discover how easy it is to get corporations to pay you for simple access to assets you've already built (hint: you're likely only 3 shifts away from this new revenue)

2. Get out of the "profit trap" so you're not in a perpetual state of launching new products or services and getting new customers in your funnel

3. Move away from proposals and move you towards positioning; placing your brand in a strong position so you can get sponsor's attention and have confidence speaking to anyone in the company, no matter their title

Before we get into how you take advantage of this new money, let's discuss why corporations NEED to spend money with influencers like you and a little insight into how they think.

Due to commercial avoiding technology and the massive amounts of information being made available online, traditional advertising and marketing is no longer effective for corporations.

Let's face it, when is the last time you watched television in real time?

Why?

Because you want to fast forward through the commercials (that, and you were likely busy when the show aired originally). And with all of the digital advertising while we're surfing the web or scrolling through our favorite social media platform, it's become habit for us to ignore those messages as well.

So as you can see, big companies are left looking for ways to get in front of potential consumers in a way that can break through the noise in the marketplace.

That's where you as an influencer, and your brand come in. Corporations have budgets and will PAY to have access to the audience that knows, likes and trusts you, is coming to you for advice, and is buying from you!

(**Side Note:** a recent study revealed that 83% of consumers take action because of trusted recommendations and 92% of consumers trust an influencer over an advertisement or traditional celebrity endorsement)

Partnering with you makes corporation's job easier, helps them sell more of their own products and services, and gets their message out into the world in unique and exciting ways that frankly they cannot accomplish in-house.

In short, sponsorship (corporations also consider sponsorship to be a form of influencer marketing in recent years) helps them solve a problem. A problem they are willing to invest handsomely in.

In 2017, 86% of corporate advertising and marketing executives utilized sponsorship and influencer marketing, 94% of whom found it to be effective.

In 2018 it shows no signs of slowing down, with 48% of advertisers and marketers planning to increase their sponsorship and influencer marketing budget, compared to only 4% who plan to decrease it.

Hopefully at this point you need no further convincing that you're leaving money on the table in your business if you're not making the time to tap into the power and leverage of corporate sponsorship.

I've worked in the corporate sponsor industry for 8 years, on both the corporate side providing training for how they best work with influencers and on the agency side, securing sponsors for my clients.

I know what corporations want, what will turn them away, and what they're willing to pay BIG DOLLARS for. That's why I've had the honor of working with major influencers like Steve Harvey, Lisa Nichols and The Susan G. Komen Foundation to micro-influencers who were only known in their niche, and guess what?

Being sponsor ready is possible if you do a few things right. The framework I'm about to walk you through will work for both the massively known and the little known influencers.

BRAIN STOP: Take a moment of silence and consider…

What would you have done differently last year if you had an additional $50,000 from a corporate sponsor?

Get feedback and advanced strategies by joining Sponsorship Magnet at www.becomeasponsorshipmagnet.com

"Building relationships before you're ready will shorten the sale when you are."

~Shayna Rattler

Chapter 3
How Sponsorable Are You?
(Take The Test)

Before I share the tried and true strategies that have enabled my clients to create hundreds of key partnerships and millions of dollars in profits, let's do a quick assessment to determine how sponsorable your brand is.

Imagine for a moment you get a call from a major corporation and they say, "Hey we have $100,000 in sponsorship dollars we're looking to spend with an influencer who serves (insert your target market). We'd like to set up a meeting to see if your brand is a good fit for this opportunity."

How confident are you that you will be able to meet their needs and requirements?

There are many things a corporate sponsor is going to expect for this level of sponsorship and what you need to have in place, but I'll cover the primary ones for now.

I'm going to walk you through the **Brand Asset Assessment** I use with clients. I want you to rate your brand on the following assets, using a 1-5 scale, with 5 being "I'm ready to rock and roll, show me the money," and 1 being, "call 9-1-1 because I haven't even thought about this area of my business and I'm going to have to shut everything down to build it."

Brand Asset	Score
Clear, defined target market (including demographics, psychographics and spending habits)	_____
Publish consistent content	_____
Social Media Presence (with at least 5k followers per platform that are engaging)	_____
3-5 ways to serve target market (including products, services, webinars, summits, live events)	_____
3rd Party Validation (including testimonials, media, books and awards)	_____
Responsive Email List (opening consistently).	_____
Engaging Content (including blogs, newsletters virtual summits/challenges)	_____
Steady stream of clients (generating at least $100k per year)	_____
Photos/Videos of you engaging with your audience	_____
Past Performance (including speaking gigs and previous corporate sponsors/clients)	_____

Access to community outlets and
other influencers/partners.   _____

Warm Relationships with Corporate
Decision Makers   _____

Now, tally up the results. How did you score out of possible score of 60?

If you scored **45 or higher**, you are ready NOW to get your proposal together and walk right up to corporate offices and have checks handed to you!

My client Sheri R., a motivational speaker in business for 4 years, scored 50 and she secured $70,000 in cash sponsorship from a Fortune 500 company and a clothing in-kind sponsor for her 5-city speaking tour.

If you scored **less than 45**, now that you know your "Point A," you can now focus on building your assets to become more attractive to corporate sponsors, WHILE you're learning and implementing the rest of the process it takes to get them to say yes.

My client Jonathan D, a community activist in his second year of business, scored 25 but was still able to secure $15,000 in cash sponsorship from his local bank and personal insurance company for his annual awards banquet. One year later he's now in negotiation with two national companies for a potential $25,000 and $40,000 cash sponsorship for his private Facebook group, group coaching program, and two-day conference.

Don't be discouraged if you score less than 45. Get excited because now you know where your opportunities for improvement exist and how you can set yourself up for this new money. This new revenue stream is easy to take advantage of when you get clearer on what is going to make you the most attractive to corporate sponsors.

Regardless of where you scored on the **Brand Asset Assessment**, you are just 3 shifts away from this new revenue!

I teach what I refer to as the Sponsorship Magnet Method™, and it is proven for getting corporate sponsors to fund your small business.

It includes the 3 P's you must master to get your brand into the top 5% of those that are getting a YES!

Let's break it down…

"Success is nothing more than a few simple disciplines practiced everyday."

~Jim Rohn

Chapter 4
Position - Showcase Your Assets

Most experts in this space tell you to create a great proposal and call on sponsors. While that's part of the process, it is not the most critical piece of the puzzle.

In fact, this is the area that makes how I teach how to get access to this free money different.

What they're not telling you is no matter how amazing your proposal may be, if you haven't positioned yourself to be the ONLY option for a potential corporate sponsor, you'll hear crickets when you attempt to get in front of them to pitch your opportunity.

Corporate sponsors are looking for the RIGHT kind of influencer and that means your number one job isn't to write the best proposal and cold email it to them, it is to position your brand as one of the only options that is perfect for them.

Do NOT skip this step! It is the most important step in the process and can be what stands between you and your big corporate payday…

Your goal during this phase is to showcase your assets from the **Brand Asset Assessment** in the most powerful way, and here are the top 3 ways you can do this, that's simple to do…

1. **You must have a clear, defined target market.**

    This seems obvious and you've heard it a thousand times in building your brand but let me tell you why it's critical when it comes to landing corporate sponsors.

    Corporations have a certain target audience they want to get their products, services and messages in front of and if your target market is not the same as the audience they want to reach this year, the sponsorship opportunity is not going to be in alignment for them and they won't even look your way.

    Secondly, there are thousands of corporations out there you could target, so narrowing your search only to those who share your target market is going to shorten the amount of time it takes you to get the ball rolling and get your check.

    In 2017, Bank of America had goals to reach small business owners who could open accounts and invest with their bank and Ford wanted to reach black females between 30-40 to purchase their automobiles. Influencers who could demonstrate they served those target markets were more likely to get the chance to pitch their sponsorship opportunity.

2. Track your online engagement.

There are two types of metrics, vanity and actionable. Vanity metrics are good for feeling awesome. These are the number of followers you have on Instagram or how many likes you have on your Facebook page.

Actionable metrics are good for taking action towards a goal. For example, open rates of your email list or the amount of leads generated from one offer.

Corporations want to know they are going to see a return on investment if they partner with you, so if your audience is not responsive or buying from you, what will make your potential sponsor think they will respond and buy from them, which is their ultimate goal.

Some of the top things to track are things like shares, comments, contest participation, and open and click through rates for your newsletters, paid ads, and webinars.

I recommend having these metrics in a spreadsheet or report format in the event you need to discuss them with a potential sponsor.

3. **Offer access to multiple ways you serve your audience.**

This is the biggest game changer in the industry these days and also what will help you stand out from your competition and make your brand scream sponsorship worthy! Think of all of the ways you serve your target market online and offline through products and services, social media, newsletters, events, etc. In the next chapter we'll explore deeper how you can give a sponsor access to these assets.

What do you need to do to increase your brand assets like your number of followers, engaging content, or other ways you serve your audience? What do you need to beef up so you can offer more exposure opportunities to your potential sponsors?

> ****For ways to do so, consider participating in my online program, Sponsorship Magnet, an online training program for the end-to-end process for what to do before, during, and after the pitch to magnetize corporate sponsors to your brand. You can learn more at www.becomeasponsorshipmagnet.com*

If you're only selling to consumers

you are in a profit trap."

~Shayna Rattler

Chapter 5
Package - Exposure Beyond An Event

The number one question I get asked by those seeking to secure corporate sponsors is "What do I offer?" followed by "What do I charge?"

Pricing your sponsorship levels and deliverables is an involved process. It varies based on many specific and individual factors so I can't do that topic justice in a book format, but I do have a proprietary **Sponsorship Investment Level Formula** that I teach in my programs and use with 1:1 clients. This formula helps to determine exactly what price points make sense based on what you are giving the sponsor access to.

So what deliverables (also known as activations) will get a potential sponsor excited?

Remember the primary reason they want to partner with you through sponsorship is to get in front of potential consumers to sell more of their products and services and to spread their messages, so the more ways you can give them exposure and visibility, the more attractive your opportunity will be.

This topic is where there is a ton of outdated information being taught in the corporate sponsorship industry AND what most people think sponsors want access to…live events.

You do NOT; I repeat do NOT have to produce a live event to get a check from a corporate sponsor!

To create the most exposure for a potential sponsor, you actually want to give them access to MORE than an event.

THIS is where sponsors can't help but to want part of the action. I refer to this strategy as a 360° Activation™, which simply means that you should include the top ways you engage your audience online and offline in your sponsorship opportunity.

Include things like exposure and visibility in your newsletters, social media, online and offline events, your programs, etc.

I discovered this strategy one day in 2014 as I was speaking with a potential sponsor for a client.

I was working hours upon hours to hear just a ton of no's and maybe's, and hopefully one yes. I was working my butt off, creating proposals, scouring LinkedIn for the right person to contact, Googling what the heck others were offering, and getting NOWHERE!

So this potential sponsor was intrigued with the client I was working for and I thought they were going to say yes, but instead they asked me a question... **"What else are they doing, because we'd like to play with that too..."**

What she meant was, "That's cool you have an event, so does everyone else. How else can we get involved with what you're doing?"

I still didn't get it, so she said, "As a corporation we're just as interested in unique ways of marketing as the small business owner. Plus we know we have to be in front of potential consumers multiple times before they take action or buy something.

So if your client has an email list, an engaged social media platform, people in programs, or a blog that has traffic to it, we'd pay for that too."

This was a HUGE game changer for me.

Because that meant that you didn't NEED an event to land corporate sponsors who are willing to write you a big check.

You just needed an engaged audience. Now if you have an event, great. That makes your opportunity even more enticing, but it's totally not necessary.

Why?

Because an engaged audience equals effective advertising or exposure opportunities for sponsors. Plus even a *world-class* event opportunity only provides the sponsor with access to the number of event attendees, for the length of the event. That is not enough impressions, or times, for the sponsor to be in front of the attendee in a way that gets them to take action.

Also, unless done properly, many event deliverables do not give the sponsor adequate ways to engage the attendees in a way that will influence a buying decision.

Think about it—how often do you walk past event sponsors and straight to lunch or the next session? Sure they're nice to talk to and they have cool free stuff on their tables, but most people don't buy from event booths or because of sponsor's logos being placed around the venue. This means that sponsors are not getting a large return on investment from event sponsorships, *as a standalone opportunity.*

And I'll let you in on a secret—*a LOT of influencers are moving away from producing big events because they're such cash suckers and they take so much time to plan.*

That's what makes this strategy so sexy. No event needed and you can apply this to what you're ALREADY DOING, which means more money with almost ZERO additional work.

Win-Win!

Implementing my 360° Activation™ strategy provides your sponsors with the most comprehensive way (maximum impressions) to get a great return on investment for their dollars. In addition to the exposure to your audience in the actual deliverable, i.e. event, program, etc., you can also give your sponsor exposure to the marketing that comes before the deliverable, which creates even more impressions.

For example, there may be 1,000 people participating in your week-long telesummit, but through the advertising and marketing for the summit, potentially thousands more will see those advertisements and thus see your sponsor's logos, messages, links, etc.

As a result, the sponsor is in front of a larger audience, more times. This is when the opportunity REALLY becomes enticing and comes with a bigger check!

So what exactly will a corporation sponsor and how do you put it together in a presentable format? Here are just a few examples of what they will sponsor:

- Blogs
- Websites
- Newsletters
- Social Media
- Online and Offline Events
- Book Tours
- Speaking Tours
- Much, much more…

I jokingly say, "If it's legal, it's sponsorable," because how you give sponsors unique and exciting, out-of-the-box exposure and engagement is limited to your imagination.

Examples of specific activation include:

- A designated area on your website where you offer tips. A company can sponsor this area and they can provide some of the tips

- Interview executives from your sponsor's company on your social media platforms

- At your events, allow sponsors the opportunity to poll the attendees for relevant insights to their products and services and offer products and services as giveaways

Bottom line; look for creative ways to give them exposure and engagement opportunities with your audience that they cannot accomplish in-house.

Also, don't be afraid to co-create the best solution by asking them what they would like to see happen. They will appreciate it and this increases your chances of success.

The next thing I want to share with you regarding packaging your opportunity is that you DO NOT need the perfect proposal.

You could write an average proposal, but if you've built a relationship with the potential sponsor and create an opportunity that stands out from the ones that have been placed before them for years, you're more likely to hear a yes than someone else's above-average proposal.

Once you position yourself to get their attention and can clearly articulate why your opportunity gives them the biggest bang for their buck, your proposal doesn't matter so much.

The proposals, or sponsorship decks as they're often called, that we create for our clients have a few essential components that I recommend you include. You can Google a sample deck, but be sure to include these elements:

- Branded cover with your potential sponsor's logo. You want it to appear customized

- Begin with lifestyle photos of you engaging with your audience before you jump to the text of the opportunity

    Buying decisions are emotional decisions, even when you're spending the money of your company, so providing these photos gives the potential sponsor an emotional connection to your brand and what you're up to in the world.

- Partner benefits. Do not just include what they get, include how it helps them reach their company goals and objectives

- Target market profile. Consider using graphs and charts to highlight your social media following, database size, audience spending habits, etc.

- Actual deliverables and investment amounts for each

By the time you get to the phase where you're sharing a deck, the potential sponsor should already have a great idea of the what, why, and how of your opportunity, so the deck becomes more of a technicality than a necessity.

Begin to make a list of the top ways you engage your audience online and offline, and then create unique ways you can create exposure and engagement for a corporate sponsor within those assets.

***A full inventory list of possible sponsorship deliverables, sample decks, investment levels and pricing strategies are included in my Sponsorship Magnet program. You can get the details and join the hundreds of others who have heard "YES" from corporate sponsors as a result of my process at www.becomeasponsorshipmagnet.com

BRAIN STOP: Take a moment of silence and consider...

What brand assets do you already have (or want to build) to better position yourself for sponsorships?

Get feedback and advanced strategies by joining Sponsorship Magnet at www.becomeasponsorshipmagnet.com

"Vision without action is a daydream.

Action without vision is a nightmare."

~Japanese Proverb

Chapter 6
Pitch – Get Past The Gatekeeper And Get In The Door

The final P in the Sponsorship Magnet Method™ is where the rubber meets the road and all of your efforts end in your not so hard earned check…

In business-to-business sales like corporate sponsorship, relationship currency is the most effective currency you can create. Selling to corporations is by far a relationship business.

Building relationships before you need them will shorten the sales cycle when you do.

Before you can pitch, you need access to the RIGHT person to pitch to. I've spent years building my corporate Rolodex using the same principles I'm outlining for you here.

These relationships have helped me bypass the most ironclad gatekeepers in the business, and be afforded the chance to work with fewer clients, while earning more.

The first steps to pitching are to know whom you should be contacting and where to find them. For the types of sponsorship that fall within the scope of what the average influencer has to offer, it is an advertising and marketing investment for the corporation.

Please note that the same title can mean various things in different companies but more than likely you're looking for decision makers in advertising and marketing, or who has brand manager or sponsorship in their title (the higher up the food chain, the better).

Before you know whom to contact you need to create a target list of the companies that are best aligned with your brand. That means the corporation has goals to reach the target market you serve, are located close to you, have sponsored brands like yours in the past, etc.

There are a couple of key things you can do to create your target list. Number one is to pay attention to the advertising and marketing that is currently in the marketplace for clues as to what particular companies are up to.

For example if an automobile manufacturer has a commercial with young black females in it, they are likely looking to target that demographic in the near future.

Additionally, if you notice a corporation is sponsoring another brand that serves your target market they are likely to sponsor a similar brand again. It is also a great idea to target companies that are located within an hour of where you are located because you are more likely to meet people who work there in an organic way or know people who work there who can make introductions to those who make the sponsorship decisions.

There are many places to find these decision makers. I recommend first exploring who you already know or have access to, as the warmer the relationship, the easier it is to get access to them.

Consider companies where you have worked in the past, done work for, or closely know someone who works there that can make introductions on your behalf. From there, good ole' Google has never let me down. In the search section, type in the name of the city you're located (or the nearest large metropolitan area) + corporate sponsors. This will produce many results but you're looking for companies that are already saying yes to brands similar to yours.

Networking at charity events/galas, museum openings, industry and association events, and anywhere else people who work for big companies hang out is a great place to spend your time to find potential sponsors. Even if the people you meet are not the direct decision makers for sponsorship, they can make introductions to the people who are responsible for those decisions.

Lastly, LinkedIn is an excellent tool for locating decision makers with the titles who can be your next corporate sponsor.

I know you're anxious to reach out to the people you discovered during your "decision maker treasure hunt," but before you do, you need to do your homework.

To create the best results and increase the chance you will actually get your foot in the door with the companies on your target list, you need to know what they care about. Your first responsibility is to have a basic idea of their goals and objectives so you can articulate why you're the best influencer to align with.

The best ways to know what they are looking to accomplish is to pay attention to their current advertising and marketing, what they have already sponsored, and to scan their website and recent press releases for these indicators.

Once you know what's in it for them, you're now ready to pitch. Pitching at this phase does not mean letting them know you ultimately want them to be your sponsor.

Pitching at this phase is to get an initial meeting with the person who has the authority to say yes so that you can explore further what they are looking to accomplish, and demonstrate that there is a business case for partnering with you to fill in the gap for reaching their desired audience.

Most importantly this first "pitch" is to show that you both bring value to the table and can help *one another*. Trust me, there is plenty of time left to sell.

I'd love to tell you that you're going to immediately get a meeting with the person you need to speak to. That's not usually the case unless you know them or have been introduced to them, which will be the smallest percentage of decision makers you reach out to.

For those you reach out to cold, I highly recommend you create an outreach plan that adds value and is not entirely based on selling or securing a meeting.

For example, if you're using phone calls, emails and LinkedIn messages to get your foot in the door, aka get your initial exploratory meeting, every point of contact should not be about why they should meet with you.

Some of those points of contact should be to provide value like sending them an article you've found that is relevant to their industry or inviting them to an upcoming event that is beneficial to them. This is the best way to stay top of mind, not get on their nerves, and get them to respond.

I've been selling to corporations for over 10 years and have had multiple people tell me the reason they agree to meet with me is that they view me as a person of value due to the ways that I bake value into my outreach plan.

Ignoring this advice will NOT get your foot in the door; in fact it will get your toes smashed!

The best way to get your initial exploratory meeting is to have a great short brand message that you use when you're networking, or in your email or LinkedIn messages, and voicemails.

The brand message helps the corporate decision maker to view you as their peer and demonstrates to them that making time in their insanely busy schedule to meet with you is worth their time.

If you are asking for an introduction, let the person who will be making the introduction know you'd love the chance to speak with the person responsible for sponsorship so you can discuss how you can help one another.

If you are reaching out to the decision maker directly, use this language:

> *"Hi Joan, I understand that you're looking to reach more (shared target audience) this year. I serve this audience in some pretty unique ways, both online and offline so it may make sense for us to chat about how we can help one another."*

Notice, I didn't say ANYTHING about sponsor my stuff, or anything even close to that. That is yet another way to get your toes smashed rather than get your foot in the door.

You do not yet have the green light to discuss your opportunity, and doing so can be extremely detrimental to your chances of getting a check because you don't yet know that it even makes sense to pitch your actual opportunity.

You still need additional information before you can advance to that step. Simply focus on getting the meeting and…

WHATEVER YOU DO, DO NOT SEND OVER YOUR SPONSORSHIP DECK

…no matter how hard they press you to "just send them some information."

The best way I've found to get around that request is to politely say,

> *"At this point I just want to learn more about what you do and what you're looking to accomplish to see if there are ways we can help one another.*
>
> *Until we explore that, I wouldn't have anything specific to send you. When would you be available for about 20 minutes to have that conversation?"*

Similar to the sponsorship pricing strategy, the actual sales script to be used is beyond what I can best explain in this book format. Once you get your initial meeting your goal is to ask them what their goals are, and explore how they best see you as a partner to reach those goals. Then and only then can should you share your specific sponsorship opportunity or your sponsorship deck.

***For access to the exact outreach plan I use with my clients, tracking tools and complete sales scripts, you'll definitely benefit from enrolling in the Sponsorship Magnet program. Meet me there at www.becomeasponsorshipmagnet.com

BRAIN STOP: Take a moment of silence and consider...

Make a list of 10 potential sponsors from your research and locate the sponsorship decision makers for each.

Also, research 3 places you can network in the next 60 days to begin to build relationships with corporate decision makers.

Get feedback and advanced strategies by joining Sponsorship Magnet at www.becomeasponsorshipmagnet.com

"You don't have to have it all figured out before you get started."

~Shayna Rattler

Chapter 7
Get Your "Heck Yes!" Check

    To bring it all together, once you have built up your brand assets you can begin your outreach plan and make your pitch. Remember not to wait until this process is complete to begin networking and building relationships.

    Look back at your score from the **Brand Asset Assessment**. That is your starting point. I've educated you on how to improve on those areas and what sponsors will be looking for. Now it's time to look at what's next.

Here are the areas of focus that need your attention:

- Maximizing/increasing brand assets
- Tracking online engagement
- Creating a visibility plan to meet potential sponsors
- Creating solid relationships with decision makers
- Creating a target sponsor list
- Creating supporting marketing materials that increase ROI
- Creating an outreach plan
- Creating an end-to-end planning process

I recommend rating yourself from 1-5 on each of these, with 5 being you've aced this area in your business and 1 being you do not have this area in place at all, so that you can prioritize your efforts and create a plan.

There is one last thing I want to share with you…a sales and marketing background may help you land corporate sponsorships, but that alone will leave you on the outside of a company with a big fat NO.

You likely know sales and marketing because you've been in business a while. You may even teach it to others, but you're competing with other influencers who also know sales and marketing.

So was I.

I spent years trying to figure out how to get corporate sponsors to pay attention to my clients when they were competing with other influencers who had also built a strong brand and had mastered the sales and marketing game.

I've spent years building relationships that get my foot in the door immediately. I've heard my share of no's and I finally got it right.

95% of people who are asking for corporate sponsorships are hearing no, but if you properly implement the Sponsorship Magnet Method™ that I've outlined for you, you'll get into the top 5% who are getting sponsored!

Bottom line is you need the right knowledge, tools, and relationships to start cashing in on these big corporate paydays.

You can go it alone or you can shorten the gap to this revenue stream by working with an expert like myself who has figured out what works, knows what to say and send, and has a rather impressive corporate Rolodex.

If you are an influencer earning up to $150,000 per year in your business, and have fair market visibility, I recommend you play full out in my Sponsorship Magnet online training program to take this corporate sponsorship journey to the max.

Join the hundreds of other influencers who are securing meetings and checks with grace and ease. You can learn more and secure your spot at www.becomeasponsorshipmagnet.com.

If you are earning more than $150,000 in revenue and have a strong market presence, you will benefit from working with me in a more individual way. We will map out the specific areas of your business and identify where all of the opportunities are and then create a strategic plan that you'll implement alongside your other strategies.

Clients who work with me in this capacity also get access to the contact information and relationships I have built over the years. **If you meet these criteria and would like to learn more, you can email my team at info@corporateattraction.com.**

Now that you have the information, please do not let this become one more thing you get excited about but do not put into action. Corporate sponsorships are by far the most lucrative revenue stream you can have in your business that requires the least amount of work.

If you want to stop self-funding your dream and increase your chances of getting to the $1 million dollar mark and beyond, then I've given you the framework for that. It's the exact framework that has allowed me to create hundreds of key partnerships and millions of dollars in profits on both sides of the corporate table.

It's time to put these 3P's to work for you and make this the year you land your first corporate sponsor.

I'm excited for what you'll create and hope to be part of that journey! You've got this! GO GET IT!

SPONSORSHIP MAGNET

In addition to this book, I have made available an extensive collection of advanced training videos, guides, tutorials, actionable tips, templates, scripts, checklists and community support at www.becomeasponsorshipmagnet.com.

Sponsorship Magnet is the only program that provides the roadmap to becoming corporate sponsor ready so you can stop self-funding your business.

No more searching. No more wasting time. No more mindless stares at a blank screen hoping someone reads your proposal. No more trying to figure it out on your own, only to get told NO!

What's included in Sponsorship Magnet:

- ★ **4 Training Videos** with Shayna to help you master what to do before, during and after the sponsor pitch.

- ★ **Unlimited Support & Guidance** in a private Facebook group where Shayna answers all of your questions and you have access to group feedback and critique of your proposals.

- ★ **Templates & Word-for-Word Scripts:** Fast track your success with these fill-in templates and scripts...

Claim your spot in Sponsorship Magnet at
www.BecomeASponsorshipMagnet.com

Chapter 8
Case Study - Steve Harvey

Steve Harvey is a well-known media star that also owns Act Like A Success, a personal and professional development company. Act Like A Success has an online membership program, a group coaching program, annual 3-day conference, a 4-city tour and engaged social media platforms.

At the second year of the conference the team decided to forego self-funding and pursue corporate sponsors. They had attempted to land sponsors in the past and heard multiple no's so they decided they didn't want to "waste any more time" on this strategy.

You would assume Steve's brand would easily get a yes from potential sponsors because of his name recognition, but only offering sponsors access and visibility at the annual conference wasn't helping his opportunity stand out from any other lesser known influencer who also had a live event.

We repositioned his opportunity in a more attractive way that included activation in the programs, conference and tour and he was able to begin to hear a yes from national companies and secure monetary sponsorships.

    His sponsors were on site at the conference and tour stops interacting with attendees, and they also were showcased in the group coaching program's private Facebook group.

Chapter 9
Case Study - Nicole Roberts Jones

Nicole Roberts Jones is a coach to women who want to get paid for what they know and create a business that brings in multiple revenue streams. She had been in business for 3 years and was planning her first conference when she came to me for help.

She knew she wanted to land corporate sponsors but did not know where to start. She also thought she was too small and corporations would not want to partner with her because she was not a nationally known brand.

Although she had only been in business a short amount of time, she had over 10,000 women in her database that she communicated with on a regular basis, a very engaged following on her Facebook page and in her private Facebook group, and programs that sold out every time she opened them.

I coached her to create a sponsorship opportunity that included her event, social media and programs. As a result she was able to secure monetary sponsorships that decreased the amount of money she spent to produce the event and she also secured in-kind sponsorships from an airline that covered the airfare for both her and her team to get to the city where her conference was being held.

Chapter 10
Case Study - Jerylen Daniels

Jerylen Daniels owned a company that takes experiential programs into schools to help students choose their career path. She ran that company while also serving as an assistant principal.

Jerylen was considering no longer offering this program due to a lack of money and the inability of the schools or parents to pay for the experience.

After taking my online course, Sponsorship Magnet, she scheduled 8 meeting with corporate sponsors and closed 3 of them, fully funding her program. This gave her the ability to take it into more schools that otherwise could not afford it.

She is now in conversation with potential sponsors to add even more schools to her calendar and to create an awards banquet. It appears that she will not have to pay for the program or the banquet out of pocket due to the amount of sponsorship revenue she projects.

Bonus Resource
*Your "Get Started Now!"
60-Day Checklist*

Below is a step-by-step checklist of everything you need to do to start becoming sponsorable. I would've given anything for this checklist when I first got started. I am **so** excited for you!

- ❏ Decide what you want
    - ❏ What is your sponsorship vision?
    - ❏ What is your sponsorship revenue goal?
    - ❏ Due Date:

- ❏ Set yourself up for success
    - ❏ Develop a comprehensive list of your target market's demographics, psychographics, behaviors, and spending habits
    - ❏ Create and practice your brand message
    - ❏ List your best assets
    - ❏ Select at least 3 assets for your sponsorship opportunity. If there are not 3, what's your plan to create them?
    - ❏ Create a content calendar so you're publishing great content consistently
    - ❏ Track your online engagement in your social media, newsletters, etc. for open rates, shares, purchases, etc.
    - ❏ Due Date:

- [ ] Do your research
    - [ ] What corporations have sponsored brands similar to yours in the past?
    - [ ] Create your ideal sponsor target list. Who do you know that works at these companies? Ask for introductions to the sponsorship decision makers
    - [ ] Who is responsible for making the sponsorship decision?
    - [ ] Create a list of places to network where employees of big companies hang out
    - [ ] Request sponsorship decision makers on LinkedIn
    - [ ] Due Date:

- [ ] Get your foot in the door
    - [ ] Use your brand message to get exploratory meetings
    - [ ] Due Date:

- [ ] Become a part of the family and get advanced resources by joining my online training program www.BecomeASponsorshipMagnet.com
    - [ ] Due Date:

About The Author

Shayna Rattler is the ultimate go-to matchmaker for top brands and influencers. As CEO of Corporate Attraction™, a global consultancy based in Dallas, Texas, Shayna has spent over a decade working with corporations, entrepreneurs and influencers of all shapes and sizes to create perfect alignment between brands and influencers for increased visibility and profit.

An expert in understanding what makes you incredibly attractive to corporate brands, Shayna also created the exclusive training program Sponsorship Magnet™, uniquely designed for business owners and influencers who want to learn how to land corporate sponsors.

Her clients have included international bestseller Lisa Nichols, media star Steve Harvey, Susan G. Komen Foundation, and big brand corporations like UPS, Delta Airlines, State Farm, and Mary Kay.

Shayna has been featured in over 250 media outlets, including the Wall Street Journal, Enterprising Women, and Black Enterprise.

Shayna is the proud mother of a son, Kielan and the daughter of super parents, Ivan and Brenda. She resides in Dallas, Texas where she is an active member of Gospel Tabernacle church. She enjoys cooking, live music and a great glass of red wine ☺